What happ

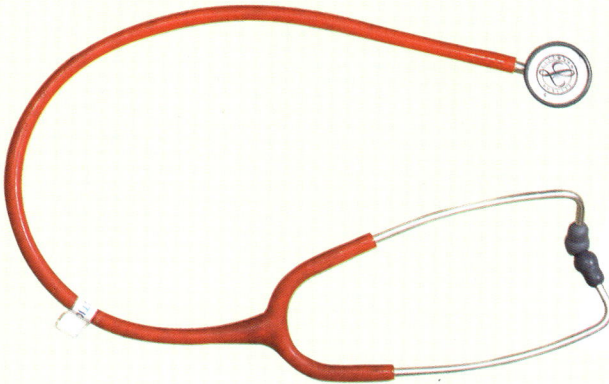

Going to the vet

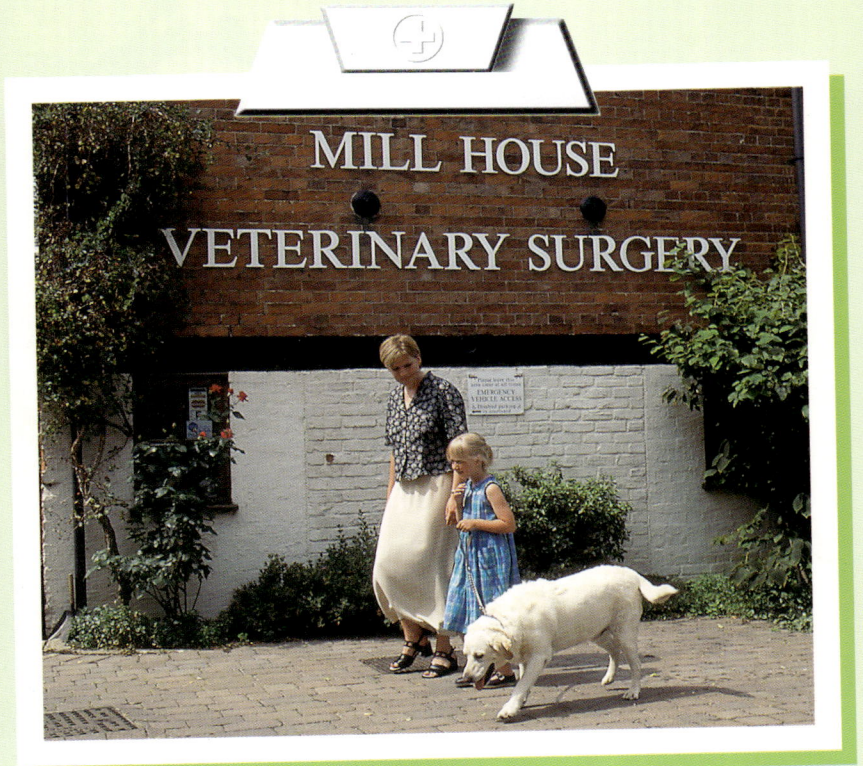

We took my dog to the vet.

Waiting for the vet

We sat in the waiting room.

The check-up

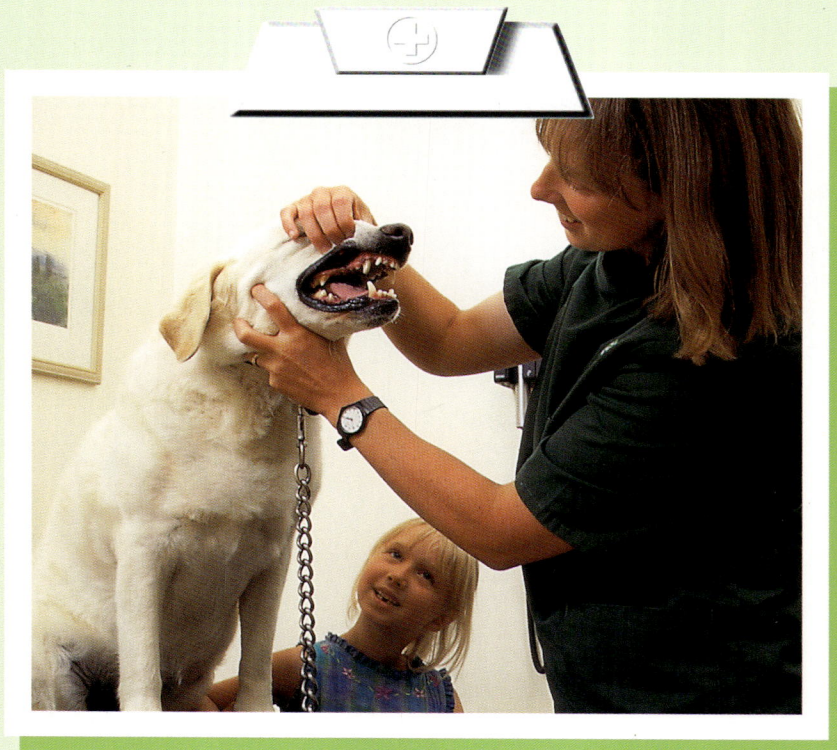

The vet looked at my dog's teeth.

She looked in my dog's ears.

She looked in my dog's eyes.

She listened to my dog's heart.

My dog was fine.